Learning Economic Theory through Role-Play

14 fun lesson ideas for Economics teachers

by George Vlachonikolis

I started out as a professional teacher seven years ago. I had just left the Army and my daughter was just weeks old. I had a PGCE but my 'economics' subject knowledge was limited and I had to read my old textbooks every evening just to get ready for the next day. Whatsmore, I hadn't really had to deal with 16+ year olds since I had been one myself (over a decade ago!). One day, only a few weeks in, I was bemoaning my students for their lack of enthusiasm. "They won't read!" I exasperated. "I spent hours looking for these articles and they just won't read them … they're just there, looking at me like they're bored out their minds". It was humiliating. But when my friend – and mentor - Simon sat me down and looked down at me with pity, he just asked me the simplest of questions: "what will they do then?"

I now understand the value of a question like that. Deliberate or not, Simon had reframed the issue for me. Instead of wallowing in my own shortcomings (what I didn't have or couldn't do) and trying to blame the students, I had to look at what resources I did have and how I could use them proactively. If the lessons I was trying weren't working, then I better look for the things that did work. Fast.

That simple question "what will they do then?" sowed the seed. And if you ask yourself the same question, the solutions for your own class(es) may be different from the ones I reached with mine. But, by engaging with that question, you might find that – like me – your planning time suddenly melts away, any lesson anxiety you might have just disappears and that your ability to function as a well-rested and happy human being improves dramatically.

Here's an example. One of my classes seemed to switch off when we did anything mathematical like *Theory of the Firm* analysis or the *Multiplier*. Many of these students were a bit shy and reluctant to talk and several of them clearly lacked any confidence in their mathematical ability. So … what will they do then? I knew that they would play games with each other. The next time a mathematical topic came up, I devised a small game that they could play in pairs. And it got them competing … which got them talking … which got them debating. The lesson started to run itself. What I found out is that my students like to argue with each other.

I used to spend hours at home researching case-studies and putting worksheets together. They weren't interested. They wanted to talk to each other and I just had to find a way to focus those conversations. This book is the result of that endeavour: finding key economic discussion points that you can let your students go. And talk.

Should you need any support with anything in this book, please email me: george.vlachonikolis@hotmail.co.uk. I like to receive feedback and I'm happy to help where I can.

Contents

1. Law of Diminishing Marginal Utility
2. Perfect Competition IN/OUT game
3. Collusive Oligopoly
4. Non-profit Max theories of the firm
5. Regulation
6. Pollution Permits
7. Economic Growth
8. Fiscal Policy
9. Monetary Policy
10. Marginal Propensity to Consume
11. Unemployment
12. Foreign Aid
13. Fair Trade
14. Capital Flight and Foreign Direct Investment

1. The Demand Curve Game

Key learning areas

Effective Demand/ Law of Diminishing Marginal Utility

The idea

- This lesson aims to introduce students to the underlying principles behind the shape of the demand curve. It gets them to simulate a particular scenario based on ultra-marathon running and then brings their ideas together.

The stuff

- Scrap paper/ notebook
- A flipchart pad and lots of pens (one pen per student or thereabouts)

The running

- There are two activities in this game. Firstly, the students will build their own individual demand curve. They do so by listening to the scenario that the teacher will read out to them, recording their own data and then plotting that data on a piece of scrap paper or notebook.
- Secondly, the students should then be placed into groups of 4-5. In their groups they should use their own individual data and plot a <u>market demand curve</u> on the flipchart.

The learning

- There are two natural 'pause' points in this lesson to discuss the learning. At the end of the first activity, it is worth going round the room and identifying the shape of the lines that everyone has drawn. Pair the students up and ask them to explain to each other why their graphs look that way. Hopefully, they will all be downward sloping but if not, the teacher should try to pick out the 'weird' ones and deconstruct them to see if the students really meant what they drew. Often, students will want to debate the gradient of the curve and whether it is straight of curved. This is useful for flagging things like elasticity in the not too distant future.
- It is important at this stage to identify the Law of Diminishing Marginal Utility too. Students should try to be encouraged to learn about the x-axis as the independent variable and the y-axis as the dependent variable; in this case – the price a consumer is willing to pay to depends on how many units s/he is consuming.
- Students normally find the second activity quite tough. In my experience, they often start to calculate averages. Instead, they can be prompted with a quick 'clue' that the limit of the x-axis is equal to the number of students multiplied by the number of rounds in the game (usually 4). The teacher should be prepared, however, to give them the first 2 co-ordinates of the line which will be different for each group (it is the highest two prices given by the members of the group. It does not matter if that it is the same person).

The Demand Curve Game: Instructions

Stage 1: Individual Demand Curve.

Ask your students to imagine they are doing a desert ultra-marathon. And they get lost. They are isolated from the pack and the support crew and run out of water. After a number of hours, they are now incredibly and on the brink of dehydration. However, there is some respite!

Out of the blue, a little old lady with a cold 250ml bottle of water has appeared and is willing to sell it to them. Ask them to think what the maximum price they would be willing to pay for that bottle would be (and to note it down).

The lady then pulls out a second bottle. Again, ask the students to think what the maximum price they would be willing to pay for that bottle would be (and to note it down).

Repeat for a third and fourth time. Thus, the students should now have 4 values.

Ask the students to plot these values on a graph (x-axis is number of bottles of water: 1st, 2nd, 3rd, 4th; y-axis is "maximum price I would be willing to pay"). In every case it should be downward sloping. This allows for an immediate follow-on discussion about the Law of Diminishing Marginal Utility. For an amusing video about the Law of Diminishing Marginal Utility, you could use show the 'egg-eating' scene from the film *Cool Hand Luke*.

In pairs, get students to discuss why their curves look different (assuming they are)? Why their numerical values are different (assuming they are)?

Ask students to think about other goods that behave like this: if you consumer more of them, the utility gradually falls away and you are prepared to pay less and less for the next unit e.g. 'jaffa cakes', soft drinks like Coca-cola.

Stage 2: Market demand curve

The market demand curve can be derived from the individual demand curves by adding up individual demand curves. One could either ask the students to derive a market demand curve for bottled water given their individual demand curves (built during the activity above) or one could use an entirely fictional scenario (such as the data given below).

	Maximum price (£) one is willing to pay for the			
	1st bottle	2nd bottle	3rd bottle	4th bottle
Mirza	100	90	30	10
Daria	50	15	5	2
James	60	40	20	5

In the scenario above, the main mistake will be in not realising that Mirza will buy the first two bottles of water in this market because he is willing to pay more for his 2nd bottle than either Daria and James are for their first. There are a few other tricky obstacles in this data set.

Movement along the line

Once the Market Demand curve has been plotted it is fairly straight-forward to ask how many bottles will be sold when the price is X, the price is Y etc … and this can lead a formal discussion about Movement along the Demand Curve.

The Demand Curve: A Worksheet

Give to students

You are going to build the Demand Curve for bottled water (in a fictional market). In this market there are only 3 buyers – Mirza, Daria and James. Their individual demand preferences are shown below.

	Maximum price (£) one is willing to pay for the			
	1st bottle	2nd bottle	3rd bottle	4th bottle
Mirza	100	90	30	10
Daria	50	15	5	2
James	60	40	20	5

Can you draw the Demand Curve for the market below?

If the price of bottled water is £90, how many bottles will be sold?

Who will be buying them?

If the price of bottled water is £10, how many bottles will be sold?

Who will be buying them?

2. The Perfect Competition In/Out Game

Keywords

Perfect Competition, Entry and Exit, Shutting Down Decision

The idea

- This activity is best employed after some teaching of perfect competition has already occurred. This lesson aims to demonstrate the process of adjustment to long-run equilibrium in a market consisting of price-taking firms.

The running

- The students should be placed into 8 groups.
- Each group is told they are a firm (A to H) and they are then given a cost of production table, which is unique to their firm. It will, of course, show that the firm has diminishing marginal returns (or, increasing marginal costs).
- The 'firms' are then told they are free to choose whether they can enter the market or not. If they enter the firm, they immediately lose their fixed/sunk costs.
- The price of the good is dependent on how many firms enter the market; the firms there are, the lower the price will be and vice versa. The handouts show what the prices will be.
- Firms can work out their 'profit-maximising' output from the price (where MC equals price) and can then work out how much profit they have made (after subtracting their fixed costs of course!).
- The winner is the team with greatest amount of profit at the end of 4 rounds.

The learning

- This is a great game for consolidating the theory behind perfect competition. Why do the firms have to accept the same market price? Is it so easy to enter/exit a market in real life? Why does the price change according to th number of firms?
- Ultimately, the game should show that those firms with the highest marginal costs do not enter the market in the long-run, and only those with the lowest marginal costs stay in. They each have the same marginal cost tables too. In addition, it should (hopefully) show that the market settles down to a regular pattern (same number of firms entering each time) after a period of volatility at the beginning – this is the definition of equilibrium
- It leads nicely to a discussion about the shutting decision and what the theory says specifically about when a firm should shut-down.

The Perfect Competition In/Out game: Teacher Instructions

The teacher to read aloud only.

Background.

You are a firm operating in a perfectly competitive market. The table I have just given out to you shows your costs of production. Do not share it with the other groups. You should fill in your Marginal Costs column now. This will important to the game.

How it works

The aim of the game is to make as much profit as possible.

In a moment, you will decide whether to enter the market or not. The price of the product depends on the number of sellers also entering the market with you, since you are all selling the same exact product. As a price-taker you will then calculate your profit-maximising level of output (where the price = marginal cost!) and then calculate your total profit/loss for each round.

Alternatively, you can choose to not enter the market. In this case, you receive zero profits for that round.

The only other option is: You join the market but if the price given is too low for your liking, you can shut-down without making anything. You will lose your fixed costs though – so you better make sure it's worth doing it. Your shutting down will not change the price for everyone else in that round.

The Perfect Competition In/Out game: Teacher's Price Table

Not to be read aloud

This is the price table depending on how many firms enter the market. Do not share this with students.

Number of firms entering the market	Market Price
1	105
2	95
3	85
4	75
5	65
6	55
7	45
8	35

The Perfect Competition In/Out game: Students' Scorecards

Cut these out and give them to your students

Firm A

Costs of production

Output	Total Costs	Marginal Costs
0	180	/
1	185	
2	200	
3	225	
4	260	
5	305	
6	360	
7	425	
8	500	
9	585	
10	680	

Enter your profit/loss for each round here:

1	
2	
3	
4	
Total	

Firm B

Costs of production

Output	Total Costs	Marginal Costs
0	120	/
1	125	
2	140	
3	165	
4	200	
5	245	
6	300	
7	365	
8	440	
9	525	
10	620	

Enter your profit/loss for each round here:

1	
2	
3	
4	
Total	

Firm C

Costs of production

Output	Total Costs	Marginal Costs
0	180	/
1	185	
2	200	
3	245	
4	300	
5	365	
6	440	
7	525	
8	620	
9	200	
10	245	

Enter your profit/loss for each round here:

1	
2	
3	
4	
Total	

Firm D

Costs of production

Output	Total Costs	Marginal Costs
0	150	/
1	155	
2	170	
3	195	
4	230	
5	275	
6	330	
7	395	
8	470	
9	555	
10	650	

Enter your profit/loss for each round here:

1	
2	
3	
4	
Total	

Firm E

Costs of production

Output	Total Costs	Marginal Costs
0	120	/
1	125	
2	140	
3	165	
4	200	
5	245	
6	300	
7	365	
8	440	
9	525	
10	620	

Enter your profit/loss for each round here:

1	
2	
3	
4	
Total	

Firm F

Costs of production

Output	Total Costs	Marginal Costs
0	150	/
1	155	
2	170	
3	195	
4	230	
5	275	
6	330	
7	395	
8	470	
9	555	
10	650	

Enter your profit/loss for each round here:

1	
2	
3	
4	
Total	

Firm G

Costs of production

Output	Total Costs	Marginal Costs
0	120	/
1	125	
2	140	
3	165	
4	200	
5	245	
6	300	
7	365	
8	440	
9	525	
10	620	

Enter your profit/loss for each round here:

1	
2	
3	
4	
Total	

Firm H

Costs of production

Output	Total Costs	Marginal Costs
0	120	/
1	125	
2	140	
3	165	
4	200	
5	245	
6	300	
7	365	
8	440	
9	525	
10	620	

Enter your profit/loss for each round here:

1	
2	
3	
4	
Total	

3. Collusive Oligopoly: the Cartel Game

Keywords

Oligopoly, Collusion, Cartel, Profit-Maximising point

The idea

- This activity can be employed at the beginning of the Oligopoly topic or after some teaching of oligopoly has already occurred. The game seeks to simulate the output decisions of firms within a collusive oligopoly/ cartel.

The stuff

- Worksheet (attached) and scrap paper.

The running

- The students should be placed groups of 4 and then each group to sit around a table. (If necessary it can be groups of 5 but the numbers for the game will need slight adjustment). Each student represents one firm in the market with an equal market share to each other. Thus, if there are 4 firms in the market they will each have 25% market share.

- The teacher will read out the instructions of the game and then the students will set about negotiating with each other and performing calculations.

- It is best for the teacher to walk around the classroom and prompt the students into performing the correct calculations where necessary and helping them to analyse their results correctly too.

- Essentially, the students are asked to calculation the 'correct' profit-maximising level of output for the market. Once they have done this, it is a straightforward deduction that they each need to produce a certain % of this total. To continue the example from above, each firm will produce 25% of the total market's output.

- Firms can then 'negotiate' with each other and agree to limit the market output but, critically, at that point they must write their actual output on a piece of paper so that the other firms cannot see. Only the teacher will calculate the total output produced by all 4 firms and this will dictate the price of the product. If the firms stick to their agreement, the 'market' will make the maximum level of profit. However, if one of the firms has 'cheated' (by producing a greater level of output) the price may fall but that individual firm may make more profit than the rest. If they all cheat, however ...

- The game lasts for 3 rounds. At the end of each round, tell the student the market price for their good and then allow them to calculate their own profits. They should keep these hidden (so that the rest of the group cannot work out who cheated!). They can then have another round of negotiations before repeating the process.

The learning

- Firstly, this is a great way to consolidate the students' understanding of the market structure diagrams. For example, can they calculate the profit-maximising level of output from real data? The teacher should ensure that by the start of the 'negotiating' round everybody is happy what the diagram looks like and why the profit-maximising level of output for the 'market' is and why.

- In the first round, some students will quickly see what the self-interested course of action whilst others will not. The teacher should try to refrain from helping some students out at this stage. At the end of the round or at the end of the game, this is the key aspect to focus on in discussion. Why is it beneficial to over-produce? Whilst it reduces price (and therefore, the total profit for the industry, it should increase profits for that individual firm!)
- If there are any games where all of the firms cheated and the price fell to such a level where all the firms made a loss, this is also worth focussing to get the students to understand why.
- If the class has already done some work of game theory, they could attempt to draw a pay-off matrix at this stage to try and illustrate the game they have just played.
- Towards the end of the discussion, it is the worth asking students how they might try to stop cheating between cartel members in the real world. And, in addition, they could be sign-posted towards articles on OPEC – upon which this game is very loosely based.

The Cartel Game: Instructions

Teacher to read aloud

Background

Each group of 4 students represents the world market for a commodity. This commodity can be tin, oil, steel – you decide. Each student within the group is a private firm. You each have an equal market to each other. So, as you're in a group of 4 you will each have a market share of 25%.

Being a private firm, you are also a profit-maximiser!

You have now come together because you believe that behaving collusively (i.e. as a cartel) is the best way to maximise profits for everyone. Due to previous meetings, you all know each other fairly well and you all know each other's production techniques. For example, you all have the same production costs which is that marginal cost of production is £2 (therefore, your marginal cost curve is horizontal at £2!!!).

How it works

First Task: You are about to have your next meeting. You and the rest of the firms in your market must decide on what output you should make (both collectively and then individually) in order to make the most amount of profit. Do you remember how to calculate the profit-maximising level of output?

Second Task: When you finish the meeting, however, you will go back to your respective countries you can choose to stick to your agreement or not. You will submit your individual level of output secretly to the teacher. Teacher will come round and collect your numbers, add them up and work out the market price. Obviously, the output there is, the lower the price will be. Once you have the market price, you will then be able work out your own profit.

Finally

The game lasts for 3 rounds. The person with the greatest amount of profit after 3 rounds wins!

The Cartel Game: Answers:

The profit-maximising level of output is **1600m units**. This is because Marginal Revenue of £2 would intersect with MC (£2) at 1600m units (half the quantity of where AR cuts MC, which is 3200m units).

As a result, each firm (in a cartel of 4) should agree to make 400m units.

To calculate the market, use the formula Price = (-0.0025 x Quantity) + 10. This is the formula of the demand curve.

To calculate profit, use the formula Profit = (Price-2) x Quantity. All I have done here is to subtract the cost per unit (£2 – since MC is constant) from the price per unit and then multiply by the sales.

Therefore, if each firm made 400m units. The price would be £6. They would each make £1600m profit!

The Cartel Game: Worksheet

Task One

The commodity market has the following demand schedule data:

Price (or Average Revenue)	Sales (in millions of units)	Marginal revenue	Firm's marginal costs
£10	0		
£9	400		
£8	800		
£7	1200		
£6	1600		
£5	2000		
£4	2400		
£3	2800		
£2	3200		
£1	3600		

From this data, you should calculate the profit-maximising level of output for the entire market.

HINT: Complete the 2 blank columns. And remember that marginal costs are constant at £2.

You could actually draw the market diagram here:

The profit-maximising level of output for the market is .... units

The profit for the entire market would be ....

If each firm makes 25% of the output, they would make .... units and .... profit each.

Task Two

Now, you play 3 rounds where you will 'negotiate' with the other firms in your cartel about how much output you will each make. But, when you finish the meeting, you will go back to your respective countries you can choose to stick to your agreement or not.

When you have decided on your output levels write them in the boxes underneath. In each round, your teacher will tell you the price (dependent on the output decisions of all firms) and then you can calculate your own profit.

Round	Output (you write this in after negotiation)	Price (you teacher will tell you this!)	Profit (you calculate this)
1			
2			
3			
		TOTAL	=

4. Non-profit maximising theories of the firm: the AGM roleplay

The AGM roleplay

Keywords

Shareholders, divorce of ownership,

The idea

- This lesson aims to simulate a very basic AGM for a small/medium limited company. The idea is that the teacher plays the role of Managing Director whilst the students play the roles of shareholders.

The stuff

- Before the roleplay, students should be given a copy of the **Letter to Shareholders**.
- If you wish, a list of possible characters is also attached. Use this if preferred.

The running

- Students should be given 5-10 minutes to read the Letter. This will provide them with a satisfactory context within which to frame the discussions later. The Letter asks the students to think about their *vision for the future* of the company and to come prepared to speak at AGM.
- The teacher (or person playing the MD) should aim to simulate an AGM run open the AGM with a brief summary of the company's recent performance and outline the options available for discussion at the AGM. This should take no more than 5mins.
- Immediately after the summary, there should be an opportunity for questions when shareholders can iron out any difficulties they have with the context. The MD may need to improvise where necessary.
- After questions, the AGM begins and each shareholder is given an opportunity to voice his/her opinion on their future vision for the company and what direction they would like the company to be steered in. One may which to consider an appropriate level of decorum at this stage – whether it is better to let the shareholders speak without interruption or allowing heckling from the other audience members.
- Once everybody has had a chance to speak, a whole group discussion may be useful at this point in order for students to challenge each other's views and try to find consensus with each other. Ultimately, the teacher should be looking for at least 2 prevailing (different) ideas that can then be used for a final vote.

The learning

- By taking on the role of a shareholder, students should be engaging with ideas such as opportunity cost and risk whilst also crunching the numbers and calculating likely profits and dividend ratios. By discussing their plans with each other it is hoped that their own analysis will be challenged and they will see the advantages and disadvantages of different courses of action. Depending on the students' suggestions during the role-play, it may be necessary here to artificially bring in other possible theories of the firm and brainstorm their advantages and disadvantages also.

Non-profit maximising theories of the firm: Letter to Shareholders
Loch Ness Air Ltd

Dear shareholder

As you know, 3 years ago you personally invested £10m in buying 10 shares (price of share = £1m) in Loch Ness Air (LNA). Since then LNA has operated airplanes from Inverness through to various local airports in Scotland and the North of England. The company is in competition with much larger rivals such as Ezyjet. However, we offer a distinctive and customer-friendly service targeted at a market segment comprising regular business travellers.

I do acknowledge the company's past financial performance has been weak and that, until now, you have not received a dividend on your shares. This year, however, I am delighted to announce that we have made a profit of £5m. The company's services have benefited from high levels of positive media reviews and sales have started to rise significantly. I believe we are now entering the growth stage of the product life cycle.

Responding to the results of our market research, I am keen to continue increasing the quality of our services. Now that the finance has become available, I would plan to refurbish the company's aircraft and to provide facilities such as more comfortable seating, freshly cooked meals and free WiFi (in-flight). Therefore, I am proposing that you, the shareholders, take only 20% of the profits for your dividend and use the remaining 80% to reinvest in the areas outlined above. I believe that if you agree to this, the reinvested profit will lead to 16.8% increase in sales next year.

I am aware that in the last few days one or two of the more vocal shareholders amongst you have publically criticised my performance as MD. I understand that you are anxious to recoup some of your investment after 2 years of not receiving a dividend but I am asking for a little more patience. If you take the entire 100% of profit this year as a dividend, I cannot guarantee the increase in sales and the lack of reinvestment may hurt the company.

	2015/16	2016/17	2017/18	Projection for 2018/19
Sales	110.5m	120.5m	146.5m	170m
Costs	140.5m	140.5m	140.5	144.5m
Profit	-30m	-20m	+5m	+25.5m

The profit figures for the last few years and my projections are shown above.

I hope you will take the time to consider my proposal which will up for a vote at the AGM. The future vision of the company and the size of your dividend is, as ever, up to you. I look forward to seeing you there.

Yours sincerely,

Angus MacGregor

Non-profit maximising theories of the firm: List of characters (optional)

Cut these out and give to students before the AGM starts.

You are Alice. Your husband died in 2008 and left you just over £10m. Your son Jim told you to invest your money rather than rush into making any rash purchases. You believe that this was the right advice but, 3 years on, you are beginning to get a bit disillusioned with the investment and thinking that you would quite like a high dividend this year (perhaps to buy a new sports car) or you may well sell your shares.

You are Boris – a Russian billionaire. You invested £10m 3 years ago on the advice of your cousin, Vladislav. You believe that business is all about money and you are very unhappy that you have not seen any money from this investment for such a long time. It is outrageous. You would like to fire the Managing Director and have him replaced. You are out to get the highest dividend possible.

You are Colin. 3 years ago you were a construction worker until one day you won £121m on the lottery. You spent most of that money on luxuries but you invested £10m on LNA on the advice of a financial advisor. You don't need any money especially quickly and you would like the company to take a more risk-taking approach by reinvesting the whole lot and try to grow rapidly – thereby increasing the potential for profit in the long-run.

You are Denise. You are a barrister in London earning upwards of £500 000 a year. 3 years ago you invested £10m in LNA shares because you thought it had potential. You have no urgency with regards to dividends payments but you do want to trust that the company's future is secure. You believe that Angus has a vision but also that Managers are easily replaceable.

You are Emma. You are the wife of an oil magnate and you essentially manage the family fortunes. You believe that Angua has had his time as the Managing Director and he has failed. You will probably sell your shares over the next 12 months so you want to make sure you get a decent dividend this year (since you have seen any for the last 2) but also that the company will be profitable again next year (otherwise if will hurt the share price).

You are Francisco – you were born into a very wealthy Italian family and your father currently sits as the Deputy Prime Minster. You have settled in Scotland though for the rugged landscapes and weather. Your real passion in life is fighting for environmental issues and you would like the company to take a much more environmental stance even if that means less profit and less dividend.

You are Georgina. You are a 56 year-old business woman who is starting to think about her retirement in 5 years time. You are not too concerned that the dividends have been low for a number of years as long as you believe the company is headed in the right direction and you will get high dividends in 3-5 years time. You believe that Angus is a good General Manager.

You are Harold van der Rich – a South African billionaire. Normally, you wouldn't bother with the AGM but you are in London on other business so you thought you would drip in. You have no urgency you're your investment money; you continue to see LNA as a good investment and you know that businesses can take 10 years to grow really profitable. You would rather see profit reinvested (though not sure if Angus has the best strategy) as long as there is some acknowledgement that dividends should be very high when the company is doing better.

You are India. You don't usually come to AGMs but thought you would today because there seems to be a lot going on in the media and in the emails that you have been sent – so you thought it would be good fun. You are prepared to listen to all sides of argument before choosing where you stand.

You are Jamaal. You don't usually come to AGMs but thought you would today because there seems to be a lot going on in the media and in the emails that you have been sent – so you thought it would be good fun. You are prepared to listen to all sides of argument before choosing where you stand.

5. Regulation

Keywords

Regulation, watchdogs,

The idea

- This role-play is designed to simulate the relationship between firms that the industry regulator. Students are pitted against each other in different scenarios to try and come to some sort of conclusion.

The stuff

- The 'character cards' provided.

The running

- Sort students into pairs.
- There are 4 scenarios. In each scenario, one student of every pair is the firm and the other student is the industry regulator. The teacher should issue the students with their relevant cards. This activity works best when all pairs are discussing the same scenario as each other. After each scenario, the students can rotate to a different partner if preferred.
- The students should be given 1-2 minutes to read over their 'character cards' and plan their questions and answers. The regulator should always be the discussion-lead as it is implied that they are the ones who have called the meeting.
- The students are given 5 minutes to speak to each other. The character cards are deliberately simple in order that the students can improvise around the scenario.
- At the end of the discussion, the regulator needs to choose how they want to proceed the scenario from this point on. They should choose their actions from a chosen list (there is one offered) or from the known regulatory powers that they have previously studies.
- Students will be prepared to justify their choices to the rest of the class.

The learning

- The power of this role-play is that students see what it is like to be on both sides of the regulatory process; both as a regulator and as a firm being regulated. In some cases, the firm may try to hide information from the regulator and/or try to manipulate the regulator's actions by framing the issues in a particular way.
- The purpose of pausing between scenarios to see what everyone else has done is to demonstrate the range of possible powers that a regulator can enact whilst also proving what a tough job the regulators have
- It might also be possible to demonstrate the concept of regulatory concept if a firm has successfully 'manipulated' a lesser punishment by not fully disclosing the truth of the issue(s).

Regulation: Roleplay character cards (1)

Cut these out and give to students

Scenario 1 – a meeting between a Rail company and the regulator.

Regulator: ORR (Office of Road and Rail)

You currently cap rail ticket prices – this was agreed 2 years ago. They have not been increased (even with inflation) since then. Rail companies have been in the news a lot recently for the following reasons:

- Customer complaints that trains are frequently late
- Customer complaints of over-crowding during peak times

Rail companies made £500m profit last year; a 1% on the year previous.

Firm: Rail Company

The regulator currently caps rail tickets but this is no good. You want to increase profits *(don't tell the regulator this!!)*. Instead, you will tell the regulator that you want them to increase the price cap rail tickets because it will enable you to:

- Increase the number of trains on the line
- Enable a better quality service

This is all rubbish. As soon as you get the money, you intend to pay shareholders a massive dividend as you do every year. You have a very good record on safety, which you could use to try and convince regulators that you are doing a good job.

Regulation: Roleplay character cards (2)

Cut these out and give to students

Scenario 2 – a meeting between an electricity company and the regulator.

OFGEM

Electricity companies have been in the news a bit recently because blackouts have become much more frequent in the UK.

There is no cap on electricity prices and energy companies have increased their prices by 10% over the last 3 years. CPI for that period was just 4.5%. Certain left-wing MPs have been calling for a price cap in the near future to protect consumers.

Electricity Company

You are actually not a true profit-maximiser – due to 'satisficing' you are somewhere between profit-maximising and community surplus maximising. You pay low dividends and shareholders see you as a safe store of wealth rather than an opportunity for fast growth.

You are angry because the Government is investing almost nothing into the country's energy infrastructure and, as a result, your production costs have increased by 15% over the last 3 years. You have actually done really well to limit your own price increases to just 10%. There have been a few blackouts recently but, again, this is not something you can do if the Government and regulator don't give you some subsidies or help to build extra capacity themselves.

Regulation: Roleplay character cards (3)

Cut these out and give to students

Scenario 3 – a meeting between a water company and the regulator.

OFWAT

Oh dear … things are going really badly with the country's water supply. Two years ago, in the North-East of the country, there was a 'bilharzia' (water-borne disease) scare for 3 weeks and 13 people died. Now in January 2017, 2 children have died from poisoning after the water companies pumped raw sewage into a local river. OFWAT has been criticised too in the national press for its inaction and MPs are calling for the Head of OFWAT to resign.

Water Company

Oh dear … things are going really badly with the country's water supply. Two years ago, in the North-East of the country, there was a 'bilharzia' (water-borne disease) scare for 3 weeks and 13 people died. Now in January 2017, 2 children have died from poisoning after the water companies pumped raw sewage into a local river. OFWAT has been criticised too in the national press for its inaction and MPs are calling for the Head of OFWAT to resign.
The truth is that the firm has been hugely x-inefficient for the last few years and people have not been paying attention to the basics. You have major problems and need to spend a lot of money now to get it back working properly. You have a very expensive company sports-car but no one needs to know about it.

Regulation: Roleplay character cards (4)

Cut these out and give to students

Scenario 4 – a meeting between a supermarket chain and the Competition and Markets Authority.

CMA

A merger between Georgeco and Simonsbury's (two of the country's biggest supermarkets) is being investigated by the CMA. The combined market share of the merged firm will be more than 50%. Rival companies such as Asrose and Waitda have complained to the CMA because they are worried that this new firm will have economies of scale that mean that they can use a predatory pricing strategy to force them out of the market. Various other supermarkets have also complained because this new firm will have so many locations that there will lots of local monopolies in out of town areas.

Georgeco and Simonsbury's

The proposed merger between your firm, Georgeco, and Simonsbury's (two of the country's biggest supermarkets) is being investigated by the CMA. The combined market share of the merged firm will be more than 50%.

Obviously, this is a profit-maximising decision and you are hopeful that the increased economies of scale will allow you to out-compete rival companies (Asrose and Waitda). You will try to convince the regulator that this is good for consumers as it will lead to lower prices and more price competition between firms. Your real aim is to use a predatory pricing strategy to outcompete many of the other smaller firms in the market *(don't tell the regulator this!!)*. You are prepared to even make a loss for 2 years to do this – but you will put prices back up when your competitors have melted away.

6. Tradeable Pollution Permits

Keywords

Negative externalities, Market failure, pollution permits

The idea

- This activity is best employed as an introduction to pollution permits (as a solution to a negative externalities market failure). This lesson aims to demonstrate how the market of pollution permits works and is actually desirable from the point of view of reducing carbon emissions and solving the demerit good problem.

The stuff

- The handout attached and a calculator.

The running

- The concept of tradeable pollution permits is often misunderstood and it is important to get students to understand a broad outline first. The following video is recommended:

http://www.youtube.com/watch?v=y7veRksc_Yk

- Alternatively, the teacher may prefer to develop a story about how different industrial firms are ordered to reduce their carbon emissions by half and getting the students to work out for themselves that some firms will find this easier than others.
- Then, the students should be put into pairs and the teacher should read through the instructions of the activity. There are two tasks.

✓ Firstly, each pair should work out the cost of reducing pollution using a quota.

✓ Secondly, the teacher needs to explain that the Government has issued price of a permit has been set for simplicity and ask them to work out: who will want to buy permits and who will want to sell; what the total new costs of reducing pollution will be to those who cut (ignore profits on trading).

This is much lower than the cost of reducing pollution using a quota, showing that the pollution has been cut in the most efficient way (question 3 of the exercise).

The Learning

As the students simulate being a firm and making the decisions, you can put the calculations up on the board. Finally ask them (still in their pairs) to come up with: 1. a summary of how these schemes work – key features etc.; 2. the main benefits and costs (as they see it) of trying to reduce emissions in this way. You can then get pairs to feed back their findings to the group and write them up on the board as they emerge.

This will enable a discussion about the likely success (or otherwise) of tradeable pollution scheme and a comparison with other policies such as indirect taxation.

Tradeable Pollution Permits: Worksheet

Give this to students

Imagine a country had 4 major power plants operating with the following emissions:

	A	B	C	D	Total
Current emissions (tonnes of CO_2)	800	2000	1267.5	1500	
Cost of reducing emissions by 1 tonne	£1	£1.50	£0.65	£2	

The Government has a target of reducing emissions by 50%. One way of doing this would be to insist that all operators reduce their emissions by half.

1) Calculate the costs of emissions reduction under this method.

2) Suppose instead that each firm is issued with a permit to emit CO_2, and that each firms is given a total number of permits equal to 50% of their current emissions levels (Therefore firm A would have 400 permits, allowing it to emit 400 tonnes of CO_2). Firms may either buy permits or sell surplus permits that they do not need – the Government sets the price at £1.25 per permit.

(a) How much pollution will each firm make under this scenario?

(b) What is the cost of pollution reduction (assuming that the permit scheme itself has no cost)?

3) You should find that the costs of emissions reduction in the second case is lower. Why is this?

4) To what extent you think that this is a good way to control emissions – identify points for and against.

Tradeable Pollution Permits: Worksheet Answers

Do not give this to students

Imagine a country had 4 major power plants operating with the following emissions:

	A	B	C	D	Total
Current emissions (tonnes of CO_2)	800	2000	1267.5	1500	
Cost of reducing emissions by 1 tonne	£1	£1.50	£0.65	£2	

The Government has a target of reducing emissions by 50%. One way of doing this would be to insist that all operators reduce their emissions by half.

5) Calculate the costs of emissions reduction under this method. **400, 1500, 412, 1500 (lowering emissions by half costs £3812).**

6) Suppose instead that each firm is issued with a permit to emit CO_2, and that each firms is given a total number of permits equal to 50% of their current emissions levels (Therefore firm A would have 400 permits, allowing it to emit 400 tonnes of CO_2). Firms may either buy permits or sell surplus permits that they do not need – the Government sets the price at £1.25 per permit.

(a) How much pollution will each firm make under this scenario?

Firm A has 400 permits. It will choose to scrub itself. Sells for £640

Firm B will have 1000 permits (cheaper than scrubing itself). It would like to buy more permits. Buys for £640

Firm C has 633.8 permits. It will scrub itself. Sells 1012

Firm D has 750 permits. It wants to buy more. 1012

7. Economic Growth

Keywords

Economic Growth, technology, PPF, LRAS

The idea

- This lesson aims to simulate the discussions that would take place between various stakeholders of a new industry – in this scenario, fracking. The idea is that the students play a number of different stakeholders and, through discussion, they tease out many of the different issues regarding that industry – many of which will complement or conflict with the idea of economic growth.

The stuff

- Two handouts are attached.

The running

- A good portion of time should be spent at the beginning of the lesson to outline the process of fracking: how it works and the controversy associated with it. The following videos are recommended:
  - http://www.bbc.co.uk/newsround/17744487
  - http://www.youtube.com/watch?v=51wOisfdIPo

- There are then two tasks. Firstly, students should be directed towards an activity of identifying the advantages and disadvantages associated with fracking (these are attached). This will help to consolidate their understanding of the fracking debate and why it is such a contentious issue in the world today. The activity should take no more than 10 minutes and may generate some discussion about the process and also about the various pluses and minuses of the industry.

- Secondly, in the final 'roleplay' activity, students are given the role of a stakeholder to play. They are then asked to discuss whether or not a new fracking company should be allowed to set-up in the local area. Students could be split into groups of 3 or more (perhaps even a whole class debate) in order that they can hear the views expressed by a number of other stakeholders. Students should not disclose exactly who they are so that the others can guess the roles at the end of the game.

- At the end of the discussion, students should vote (impartially) on whether they would like the Government to encourage this new industry to the UK. And, if they do, whether they would be happy for a company to be located near to them?

The learning

- By taking on the role of various stakeholders, students should be engaging with ideas such as ethics and the external environment as well just the economic issues. Obviously the nature of the roleplay is to highlight the economic benefits of fracking such as reducing unemployment and supply-side improvements. But it is important to balance this against the potential economic costs.

- By discussing their views with each other, it is hoped that the students will see the same issue from a number of different angles and begin to evaluate the issues in terms of their relative importance. As a result, they will be able to make an informed decision about the relative merits of a 'fracking' business locating in a specific location.
- Once the overall activity is completed, the teacher might then choose to take a more holistic view of economic growth and its advantages/ disadvantages.

Economic Growth: Task one: advantages/ disadvantages

Cut out and give to students

Fracking uses huge amounts of water that mist be transported to the fracking site at a huge environmental cost	Fracking allows firms to gain access to difficult-to-reach resources of oil and gas
The fracking process has been linked to small earthquakes	Fracking might significantly boost oil production and drive down energy prices
Fracking brings up a number of land rights issues	Chemicals may escape and contaminate groundwater around the fracking site
Natural gasses from fracking are a lot cleaner than using coal as a fuel	Fracking provides jobs
Fracking out is crowding out the potential investment for more sustainable energy sources such as solar and wind	Fracking will bring about profits for firms which can then be taxed by the Government

Economics Growth: Task two: Character Cards

Cut out and give to students

An unemployed person	The owner of a gas company
The owner of the fracking company	The owner of a solar energy company
Yourself	Someone who's back garden will be disturbed
The Green Party	The water company

8. Fiscal Policy Roleplay

Keywords

Fiscal policy, taxation, Government Spending.

The idea

- This activity is best employed at the end of the fiscal policy as a way of concluding all of the learning until this point. The idea is for students to be given a case-study of Greece in 2012 (right in the middle of the Greek debt crisis) and asked to make various fiscal policy decisions.

The stuff

- All of the information attached

The running

- Students are put into groups of 2-4. They are then given the data handouts (attached). The handout is fairly self-explanatory. The groups have two task:
  - Write an overview of Greece's economic situation in 2012.
  - Explain the fiscal strategy that you would have pursued in 2012 and be able to justify it.
- This can be done in a lesson or as homework (or as a combined lesson/homework assignment). Ultimately, the main aim is for students to digest and analyse the data they are given and then to make sensible economic arguments based on their analysis. There is no right or wrong answer BUT, instead, teachers should be looking for flaws in logic or obvious mistakes in data analysis.

The Learning

- One obvious learning objective is simply with data analysis and whether or not the students can make accurate deductions from the data. Their 'solutions' to the problem can differ but their first test is to interpret 'the problem' correctly.
- Students should be able to approach their fiscal policies strategies in any way they wish – teachers should refrain from giving them too much guidance. The key in the presentation/ written report is just to make sure that the justifications are appropriate for the action. For example, decreasing the higher rate of tax might (just about)be justified from a Laffer Curve/ increased tax revenue for the Government point of view but it is unlikely to solve an income inequality problem.

Fiscal Policy Game: The Data

GREEK FINANCE MINISTER

A game for sixth-form Economists

BACKGROUND

On 21 Feb 2012, Eurozone finance ministers reached a €130bn bail-out deal for Greece. The bail-out came with tough terms, including harsh austerity measures (reduction in government spending and increasing tax rates) as well as a permanent team of monitors in Greece to ensure the terms were met.

On 17 June 2012, the Greek election resulted in a hung parliament – that is, is a state of a parliament when no single political party had an absolute majority. Antonis Samaras, the leader of the largest party (**New Democracy**) led the negotiations to try and form a new government.

After 3 days, on 20 June 2012, a new coalition government comprising of **New Democracy**, **PASOK** and **DIMAR** (2 left-leaning political parties) was formed. **Samaras** was appointed as the new **Prime Minister**. He was keen that Greece should respect **the existing bail-out conditions but that there should an attempt to renegotiate the austerity terms of the agreement at the earliest possible opportunity.**

Your task:

You are the Greek Finance Minister.

After 100 days in Government, the Greek Parliament has convened a public debate on the current economic strategy and whether or not it is time to change economic course.

As Finance Minister, you must:

- Write an overview of Greece's economic situation in 2012.
- Explain the fiscal strategy that you would have pursued in 2012 and be able to justify it.

Greek GDP last 5 years (2008-2012)

Year	GDP (US $ bn)
2008	354.5
2009	330.0
2010	299.4
2011	287.8
2012	245.7

Greek unemployment rate last 5 years (2008-2012)

Year	Unemployment rate (%)
2008	6
2009	7
2010	11
2011	14
2012	22

Greek average monthly salary last 5 years (2008 – 2012)

Year	Av. monthly salary (€)
2008	1300
2009	1320
2010	1400
2011	1380
2012	1390

Greek minimum wage (monthly)

Year	Monthly min. wage (€)
2008	770
2009	790
2010	870
2011	870
2012	880

Greek retirement age – women

Year	Retirement Age (Men)	Retirement Age (Women)
2008	57	57
2009	65	57
2010	65	60
2011	65	62
2012	65	63.5

Greek annual Fiscal Deficit last 5 years (% of GDP)

Year	% of GDP
2008	-10
2009	-15
2010	-11
2011	-10
2012	-9

Greek Debt to GDP ratio last 5 years

Year	Debt to GDP ratio
2008	109.4
2009	126.7
2010	146.2
2011	172
2012	159.6

Greek government (10Y) bond yield last 5 years

Year	10Y bond yield (%)
2008	5
2009	5
2010	6
2011	11
2012	33

9. Monetary Policy Roleplay

Keywords

Monetary Policy, interest rates

The idea

- This activity is best employed at the end of the monetary policy topic as a way of concluding all of the learning until this point. The idea is for students to simulate being the Chair of the Federal Reserve in America and responding to data given in order to make informed choices about monetary policies.

The stuff

- All of the information attached

The running

- Students are put into groups of 2-4.
- They are 6 pieces of data (at random) from the data handout.
- They then have 6 minutes to analyse the data and come up with a monetary policy solution, as if they were the Chair of the Fed
- Students will present their findings to the rest of the class before the role-play is reset and the group is given another set of (random) data.
- This role-play works well if all groups are given the same data sets. This way they can present their solutions and compare with each other.

The Learning

- Like the Fiscal Policy role-play, the obvious learning objective is simply with data analysis. The difference here is that the data is much more limited and can (potentially) be contradictory. But that's real-life. The best students will try to illustrate their data using AD/AS diagrams and then attempt to solve 'the problem'. Their 'solutions' to the problem can differ but their first test is to interpret 'the problem' correctly.
- Students should be able to approach their monetary policies strategies in any way they wish. The obvious feature of monetary policy as A-Level is interest rates but students should be encouraged to use Quantitative Easing, Capital controls and reserve requirements if they are content to.
- Like the Fiscal Policy role-play, the key in the presentation is just to make sure that the justifications are appropriate for the action.
- If the different groups are given the same data, there is a clear opportunity to compare the solutions of each group. This way the students themselves can begin to evaluate the likely effectiveness of each other's policies.

Monetary Policy Role-play: Data

Cut out and give one from each row (at random) to each group.

#			
1	Inflation (3yr history)	Inflation (3yr history)	Inflation (3yr history)
2	Forecast: Growth GDP to rise by 2% next year. Driven by high spending.	Forecast: Growth GDP to grow by 1.5%. Spending to remain unchanged.	Forecast: Growth GDP growth of just 0.5% next year. Savings ratio begins to increase.
3	Forecast: Trade New trade deals to drive an increase in exports.	Forecast: Trade US Dollar under-valued. Exports are booming.	Forecast: Trade US Dollar over-valued. Exports struggling. Imports to rise.
4	Government Corporation tax reduced and business regulation eased.	Government Budget cuts to hit hard as austerity programme kicks in.	Government Commitment to build lots more social housing. Minimum wage increases to $10 an hour.
5	World Asian economies to slow-down next year. European economies paralysed by Brexit talks.	World Stock-market crashes in China and Japan. Canada and Mexico see little growth.	World China sees record growth.
6	Other Household debt as a % of GDP hits record high	Other Oil prices to see a small fall (2%).	Other Oil prices see a large (10%) rise.

10. The Marginal Propensity to Consume Game

Keywords

Consumption, Marginal Propensity to Consume

The idea

- This activity attempts to simulate the experience of being at a fair with a different budget (income) each time. The students should be able to derive a graph of Income v Spending with their data.

The stuff

- Handouts (attached)

The running

- Students work through this activity individually.
- The teacher reads the instructions to the class, essentially setting the context to game which is are going to a fair with a fixed budget (income). They are given a list of the things they can buy at the fair with their money. They should make a list of things they wish to buy and calculate the total costs. They do not have to spend all of their money.
- The scenario is repeated 5 more times, each time the students is given an increased budget. Each time, they work out what they will spend their money on and the total cost. It is important to note that each 'repeat' is a fresh game and the students have not already consumed the goods/services from any previous round.
- After the 6 rounds, the students will have a table of data from which they can now plot a graph of income v consumption which will allows for a discussion on the relationship.

The learning

- The relationship between income and consumption is an important concept to get right early on – particularly the fact that it is not a linear function. The game *should* identify this fact for the students and it is worth a discussion as to why this is the case (that as income increases, people have satisfied their wants and needs more, and choose to spend more and more of their higher income)
- This can then lead onto a discussion about the marginal propensity to consume (and using the graph to calculate it). Also, the concepts of average propensity to consume and marginal propensity to save are obvious concepts that a teacher could go into from here.
- It is worth thinking about how this also links to future macro topics such as fiscal policy – for example, if the Government reduces incomes tax for all earners, is this likely to increase consumption for all earners to the same extent?

Marginal Propensity to Consume game: Instructions

To be read aloud

Background

I want you to imagine that you are going to the fair with your friends for the afternoon. Your parents have given you allowance for the day and this is the only money you have access to all day. You cannot withdraw money from a cash-machine etc …

How it works

In the first round. You will have an allowance of just £5. I want you look at the list of things you can buy at the fair and choose what to spend your money on. You do not have to spend all of your money but you can if you wish. Once you have decided, calculate the total amount that you have spent (make sure it is not above your budget!) and note it down.

There will 5 more rounds after this. There is no competition here, you just need to think about your own personal preferences and what you would like to spend your money on. The game is reset each time, so – for example – the items you bought in round one have not already been consumed at the start of round 2. Round 2 is a fresh start, as is all future rounds.

At the end of each round, calculate the total amount that you have spent and note it down.

Finally …

You will be asked to plot this data at the end.

Do not read aloud

round	budget
1	£5
2	£10
3	£20
4	£40
5	£80
6	£320

Marginal Propensity to Consume: Student Worksheet

This is the Price List at the fair:

What will you buy?

Rides	**Food**	**Games**
Roller Coaster - £2	Hot Dog - £2	Coconut Shy - £1
Ghost Train - £2	Burger - £2	Basketball - £2
Log Flume - £2	Kebab - £5	Hook a Duck - £1
Dodgems - £1.50	Chips – 50p	Tombola - £1
Carousel – 50p	Pizza - £5	Arcade - £2
Bungey Jump - £5	Ice Cream - £1	Air Hockey - £1
Spinning Tea Cups - £2	Candy Floss - £2	Roulette Wheel - £5
Big Wheel - £2	Chocolate – 50p	VR experience - £3

At the end of each round, complete the relevant box in this table.

Round	Budget (your teacher will give you these)	Total Spending in the round (you fill this in in!)
1	£5	
2		
3		
4		
5		
6		

At the end of the game, plot your data here.

Spending

Budget (Income)

11. The Job Centre roleplay

Keywords

Unemployment, Welfare, Measures of unemployment, Claimant Count

The idea

- This lesson aims to build an understanding of one of the main measures of unemployment (that Claimant Count) by forcing the students to simulate the experience of working at a Job Centre.

The stuff

- Character cards

The running

Students are put into pairs. The students are told they are in charge of determining eligibility for Job Seekers' Allowance (unemployment benefit!).

They are then given the character list which has 25 people (and some very limited info). In the first round, the students should not told anything about the eligibility criteria for JSA – just that they should give it to whoever they believe is worthy.

Once, that round is over. The students can be shown the JSA criteria here: https://www.gov.uk/jobseekers-allowance/eligibility

They should then repeat the exercise.

The learning

In the first round, it is quite interesting to see what the students think about who should get JSA and why. It is worth having a discussion here to pull out what the students consider to be worthy criteria and, as an extension, they can devise their own definition of unemployment or JSA criteria.

At the end of this discussion, it is key is to then look the actual JSA criteria and compare it with their views. And whether or not they think it is fit for purpose.

The purpose the second round is then to apply the actual criteria and see the differences.

Interesting extensions to this activity might be to compare the JSA criteria with the LFS unemployment definition (and repeat the exercise for a third time) or it might be to look at other aspects of the Government's web-page – for example to see how much JSA actually is and whether or not the students agree with this.

A final point of discussion to begin to draw out the different types of unemployment. In several of the character cards, the people are unemployed for different reasons. The teacher can use this as a jump-off point to start defining the various types of unemployment.

Job-Centre roleplay: Handout

You are a mid-level manager at the Job Centre. You are schedules to meet 16 different people today, each of whom are claiming JSA. Your task is to approve or reject their application (with justification!). You only have limited information in some cases but you should make a decision even so.

Name	Approve Reject	Intentionally blank
	(put a tick in the relevant box)	

Job Centre Role-play: Characters

1. Anastasia worked 36 hours last week as a lorry driver. She was fired on Friday because the firm is seeing a reduction in demand.

2. Boris lost his job as a secretary three months ago. Every week he visits an employment agency to try to find a new job, which he would be able to start immediately

3. Charlotte has no job because she is at Oxford University studying Economics and Management.

4. Denzil looks after his one-year-old son. He neither holds a job, nor wants a job.

5. Erica has no job from which she receives any pay or profit. However, she helps in her parents' shop for around 20 hours per week

6. Francesco couldn't find a job last year because he had no skills. He is currently receiving training at a local hairdresser. This is being partly paid for by the Government. He works 28 hours a week and goes to college for 1 day per week

7. George lost his job as a teacher and looks for work each week. His wife is still working in her job as an investor banker and earns over £100k a year.

8. Hermione is out of work, but stopped looking for new jobs a year ago as she does not believe any jobs are available

9. Iris has no job because she is aged 3 and busy playing lego at home.

10. Johnno is 25. He was recently fired by a well-known coffee franchise after National Minimum wages went up and they could no longer afford to keep him on. Johnno has just over £20 000 in savings which his parents gave him when he turned 18.

11. Katherine retired from her job last year and is claiming her state pension. She is still looking for part-time work.

12. Lemar is a freelance journalist. He submits stories each week, but is paid in lumps every month or so. Last month he received no payments, even though he submitted copy

13. Mark is on a zero-hours contract with a well-know sports retailer. Sadly, he only had 4 paid hours of work last week and just 2 hours the week before that.

14. Nina previously worked as middle-manager for a well-known car manufacturer. She lost her job as the company relocated to China and she didn't want to move. Nina wants another job but she won't accept anything below £60 000 a year.

15. Ollie has finished school but isn't starting Uni for 12 months. He wants a temporary job to save money for travelling but figured he could claim for JSA whilst he was waiting.

16. Paola worked as a check-out assistant at a well-known supermarket until she was replaced by the automated self-service machines. She is a Portuguese citizen.

12. The Foreign Aid Debate

Keywords

Development, Foreign Aid, Opportunity Cost

The idea

- Much like the Fracking activity, this lesson aims to simulate the debate that would take place between various stakeholders in the foreign aid debate – both recipients and donors. The idea is that the students play a number of different stakeholders and, through discussion, they tease out many of the different issues regarding the issue.

The stuff

- Character cards attached.

The running

- Although you run straight into the debate, it is recommended that some time is spent at the beginning of the lesson to outline the foreign aid debate: how it works and the controversy associated with it. The following videos are recommended:
  - https://www.youtube.com/watch?v=FJntu9ZIWDs
  - https://www.youtube.com/watch?v=HIPvIQOCfAQ
- Students could be split into groups of 3 or more (perhaps even a whole class debate)
- Students are then a character card. They are given a few minutes to consider what this person is likely to believe/argue for in terms of the foreign aid debate. Then, after that time, they can debate between themselves.
- After 5 minutes of discussion, the groups can be shifted around or the character darsd swapped over to different people and the same process repeated.

The learning

- At the end of discussion, it is important to highlight the key arguments as the students see them. This can take the form of writing a list on the whiteboard so that it highlights all of the arguments to the students.
- Then a separate discussion could be formed where students now are giving their 'real' opinion (without the limitations of the character cards!) with the idea of evaluating whether or not the UK should give less foreign aid to developing countries. One way to do this is to rank the list of factors in order of importance.
- This can be followed up by asking the students to research examples which prove (or disprove the points) on the board or they can be asked to mark a model essay (attached) to see if they agree with the points made, if they would add any etc …

Foreign Aid Debate: Character Cards

Cut out and give to students

A parent of a cancer sufferer who can't get operation paid for on the NHS	A UK manufacturer who used to get Government subsidies but they have now been taken away due to austerity
The Government of a developing country	The UK Government
The CEO of a charity in the developing world	A citizen in an underdeveloped country who believes his/her Government is highly corrupt
A citizen in an underdeveloped country who has seen some benefits from foreign aid	A publicity seeking rock-star

Foreign Aid: Mark the essay task

Evaluate the possible microeconomic and macroeconomic effects of a cut in the UK's foreign aid budget on both the UK economy and the economies of recipient countries (25)

The UK government has pledged to commit 0.7% of its GDP to foreign aid. In 2016, this amounted to £12.2bn. The UK is one of only six countries who met the 0.7% target last year. As a result, this policy has become increasingly controversial.

Foreign aid should increase the level of economic development within a recipient country. Any injection of income into the circular flow will lead to an increase in economic growth and greater opportunities for job creation. For example, in Ghana, foreign aid has been used to develop the Millennium Villages project. The money has helped to build educational facilities and pay for trained staff to deliver vocational training to local farmers. This has the effect of increasing the level of human capital within Ghana, increasing productivity and, in turn, lowering costs of production (as best practice is now shared quicker and wider). As a result, prices should fall and goods should become more competitive in international markets. An increase in exports will further increase AD.

Given that under-developed countries should have a higher MPC too (because they are starting from a low income base), the multiplier effect from these AD increases is also likely to be higher. Consequently, any reduction in foreign aid from the donor country (such as the UK) would cause this a dramatic slow-down in economic growth. Unemployment may start to rise and it may send that recipient country into recession. This is particularly true for those countries that receive a lot of aid and, to a large extent, have become dependent on it. In 2012, 28.4% of Malawi's GDP came from foreign aid. This means that the government and a large portion of the private sector completely rely on foreign aid for revenue and, if that aid is to be pulled away, the economy would collapse into recession.

Much of the support for cutting the aid budget centres around a general argument that the money spent overseas is needed at home. The UK media, for example, constantly reports on the falling standards of UK public goods such as hospitals and schools. Thus, UK citizens might well argue that their needs should be the priority for the UK Government; to cut the foreign aid budget would 'free up' money to be spent elsewhere in the economy.

That said, any money spend in an under-developed country will have a far greater effect than of the same amount of money is spent in the UK. This is because, in poorer areas, any extra income can go a long way. The great strides that have been made in curbing diseases like polio and malaria are testament to this. Given the fact that it is only 0.7% of the UK's GDP, this money could be seen as doing a lot more good overseas than back in the UK. In addition, spending that money now may also curb greater spending later. When countries collapse into recession – as they might do, if their aid budget is cut - it can create a breeding ground for extremist political parties and leaders. The developing world is often plagued political instability, insurgency, civil war and even genocide for these reasons. These events may then create a greater financial burden for the UK. The current migrant crisis, for example, is a having a very serious drain on the Government's budget.

In conclusion, foreign aid can to be useful in a number of different ways. It can directly improve the standard of living in developing countries by solving immediate crises such as food/water shortages and epidemics (e.g. Ebola) but also in the longer term if you look at the Millenium Villages projects in Ghana. Cutting aid risks pushing those under-developed countries into recession, into poverty, into war and maybe even into a humanitarian crisis. That said, the money saved by cutting the aid budget could 'free up' the Government to spend more money in other areas in the UK and, given that the country, has a precarious economic situation at present, they could well be a timely fiscal boost.

13. The Fair Trade Game

Keywords

Development, Fair Trade, Economic Growth, Specialisation

The Idea

- This activity aims to simulate the production process of a banana – from its growth in an underdeveloped country such as Colombia to its retail in a developed country such as the UK.

The stuff

- The handout provided
- A banana often works as a good prop at the front of the class (preferably with a fair trade sticker on it!)

The running

- The first thing to do is reach a consensus with the class about how much a single banana costs in the supermarket (say 30p).
- The activity can be run with no introduction and the students can work out most of the learning points as they go along. From experience, however, the lesson is often best preceded by a short video(s) of the banana industry. Two good examples are given here:
  - https://www.youtube.com/watch?v=pPR5gHXBilg
  - http://www.youtube.com/watch?v=CAbFLBM6uHM
- To run the activity, students should be split into 5 groups. Each group is then given a character card (attached). The students should be given 5 minutes or so to read their card and then make notes. The teacher should write all of the 'characters' on the board.
- The activity takes the form of a debate where each group presents on the reasons why they are vital to production process and deserve a decent percentage of the selling price of 30p. They should also state what they believe the other characters are worth.
- Invariably, once all the groups have presented their case – the accumulated total that the groups are asking for will be greater than 30p. Then, a whole class discussion can ensure where all the 'characters' can discuss they want to distribute the money. Ultimately, the class is aiming to agree on a consensus on the distribution.
- If it helps, after the discussions are well underway, students can stop playing as their characters and discuss the issue as per their 'real' opinions. At the end of the discussion, the students can see for themselves what the 'correct' answer is on the handout provided.

The learning

- The first major learning objective here is to identify the problems for developing countries that sell primary products like bananas (that is, the supermarkets in the developed world make most of the profit and the workers see very little for their labour). This may lead on to a discussion about primary product dependency or the Prebish-Singer hypothesis (or a consolidation of previous learning).

- The next point is to focus in on what Fair Trade is and how the process works (i.e. how it can better the situation for workers and the country producing bananas). Moreover, it also needs to link back to development issues and how Fair Trade can aid development and economic growth. There is a case-study on the WindWard islands provided.

Fair Trade: Character Cards

Banana Worker

You work for anything up to 14 hours per day. It is hard physical labour in hot conditions. Some of the different roles that you perform are:

- Washing bananas – you will have your hands in water all day.
- Cutting bananas – you will have to carry heavy loads on your back.
- Applying fertilisers and pesticides – can lead to health risks such as cancer and other diseases.

You have an ill son at home who needs looking after and medical treatment that you cannot really afford. Your other children are not old enough to work yet but the only real employment possibility for them in the future is with the banana industry (it is a monopsony!). Right now you desperately want them to go to school but, again, you cannot afford it. All of your money goes on food and essentials.

Banana Company

You run the business operation in the country. You have all the fixed costs such as factory space, land rents, automated machinery, tools etc … and the variable costs such as expensive pesticides and fuel for transportation. The other major cost to your business is wastage. There are huge regulations in your main markets of North America and Europe that your bananas have to meet and the consumers in those countries are notoriously picky – often demanding the best banana.

You have queues of people trying to get a job at your factory all day long, so you see the workers are very replaceable. To that end, you expect them to work hard every day – otherwise you are quite content to fire them and hire someone else.

Shipping

Your job is to take delivery of the bananas in country and then ship them to the major ports of North America and Europe. Big cargo ships are very expensive to buy, to staff and to keep in working order. In addition, the fuel costs are massive – bear in mind that a trip from South America to Europe can take over a month!

The other fees you need to incur are port fees, refrigeration costs (bananas need to be kept cool whilst they travel) and insurance. All in all, this is a very expensive business. There are plenty of other rival shipping businesses out there but they all charge more or less the same price – the profit margins are not that high!

Supermarket

You take delivery of the bananas when they arrive at the port. You have to pay any import taxes that are due here. Before the bananas hit the shelves though, they need to be ripened. This is done in large ripening centres at the supermarket warehouse. This, again, costs money! From the warehouse, your staff then deliver the bananas to the various supermarkets round the country. Whilst you have economies of scale, this is still a hugely expensive task in terms of fuel.

You have to charge a lot for a banana because, ultimately, you take all the risk. If the consumers don't like the bananas in stock, then you face a loss because you have already paid for them. If any are left on the shelf at the end of the day – again, this is wasted money. Therefore, you need high profit margins per bananas to make up for the ones that don't get eaten.

Fair Trade: Handout

Give to students

Read your character card.

How much of the 30p should you get for the work that you do? Make your notes here:

....
....
....
....
....
....
....
....

Fair Trade Game: Teacher Notes

	Worker	Company	Shipping	Supermarket
How much do you think they should get?				
Reality (source: cafod.org.uk)	1p	5p	4p	20p

Fair Trade Game: Post-Game article: Instructions

After playing the Fair Trade Game, ask students to read this article and explain how Fair Trade can help to overcome the problems associated in the game.

Edited article from https://geographyalevelslc.files.wordpress.com/.../windward-islands-farmers-and-bana...

How Fair Trade has helped the Windward Islands

Windward Islands: Dominica, St Lucia, and St Vincent

Background

The banana trade has been crucial to the national economies of the Windward Islands since it was established more than 50 years ago by the former British colonial power to supply the UK market. Bananas have provided a direct living for thousands of small-scale producers, accounting for up to 50% of the Windward Islands' total export revenue. The Windward Islands were hit hard after the WTO ruling against their links to the UK and Europe in the Banana Wars Trade War.

Fairtrade

Of the 4,000 remaining banana growers in the Windward Islands approximately 3,400 are members of the 48 Fairtrade groups across Dominica, St Lucia and St Vincent.

The first small consignment of Fairtrade bananas from the Windwards was shipped to the UK in 2000. Since then volumes have grown to nearly 42,000 tonnes and the percentage of Windward Islands bananas sold to the Fairtrade market has grown from 30% in 2004 to over 90% in 2009.

Fairtrade has helped banana farmers to strengthen their organisations and regain confidence in the banana industry, which had been eroded by the long-term decline. Traditionally the farmers sold their crop to banana companies on the Islands who cut into farmers' profits and provided few services in return. But in the face of strong resistance from banana companies, WINFA is now responsible for the whole supply chain up to export. It provides services such as the supply of fertiliser, pest and disease control, and agricultural extension, at a significantly reduced cost to the farmers. Over 100 new staff have been hired in the Islands, technical staff trained, and payment and pest control departments created.

It is only by selling their produce as Fairtrade – and receiving the Fairtrade price and premium – that the banana farmers of the Windward Islands have been able, so far, to remain in the market. The challenge now is to maintain sales to the UK Fairtrade banana market and to develop Fairtrade, regional, and other markets for additional fresh fruit such as mangoes and coconuts, along with juices and processed fruit products from the Islands. And for those farmers unable to compete in the new environment, ways must be found to diversify away from agricultural production.

As well as the Fairtrade minimum price, WINFA receives a Fairtrade premium of US$1.00 a box to invest in a wide range of business and community improvements, selected by the farmers. Examples include:

Examples of Fairtrade Premium Use across the Islands

Hurricane Disaster Fund

When Hurricane Dean wiped out banana production in Dominica in 2007 and caused widespread damage in St Lucia and St Vincent, farmers were able to invest premium money in quickly getting back into production by funding field rehabilitation, replanting of banana trees, provision of fertilizers, and paying labour costs.

Subsidised Fertilizers

With fuel prices rising worldwide, fertilizer prices more than doubled in 2008. Over US$200,000 was used for the bulk purchase of fertilizer without which farm yields would have been seriously compromised.

Examples of Fairtrade Premium Use in Dominica

When the medical store at the hospital in Roseau burnt down the opportunity was taken to replace it with a sturdy hurricane-proof building,

A new school bus was purchased to take village children to the school in Calibishie,

A new pre-school was built adjoining the primary school in Bense.

Examples of Fairtrade Premium Use in St Lucia

A banana ripening centre is under development to expand sales to local market,

Farmers and workers receive an annual healthcare allowance of up to US$370 to cover GP visits, medicines, and costs of surgery or other treatment,

Sterilizing equipment was donated to Dennery Hospital,

Because few farmers have access to a pension, a retirement fund was set up to provide a lump sum payment on retirement,

A water project supplies clean water to 120 villagers in Rosalie,

A range of community projects were funded including improvements to farm roads, tree planting, bus shelters, equipment for a retirement home, and sponsorship of sporting activities.

Examples of Fairtrade Premium Use in St Vincent

A new school bus was purchased for children in North Windward,

Refurbishment of community centres to enable the community to make greater use of them,

Improvement of feeder roads and bridges to give banana farmers better access to their fields and benefit all farmers located along these roads,

Purchase of two computers for a secondary school in Overland,

Support for three nurseries with equipment enabling children to rest after lunch. Purchase of toys, storybooks and tape recorders,

Purchase of a nebulizer for respiratory patients at a rural clinic in the north of the island,

Construction of two bus shelters to protect passengers from the sun and rain.

14. Investment Game: Capital Flight and FDI

Keywords

Investment, Capital Flight, FDI

The idea

This lesson aims to improve students' appreciation of investment risks. The idea is that students are given a notional sum of money to invest and they have a number of options in which to invest that money. In so doing, they are exposed to alternative forms of investment (the opportunity cost of investing in a business say) and also the level of risk involved in each of those investments.

The Stuff

Handout (provided)

One dice (or virtual dice, which can be found on the internet)

The running

Students can play the game in groups, pairs or individually (from now we will call them 'players'). Each player should be given the handout provided. This explains the context of the game and it is recommended that this is read out loud at the beginning so that everyone can follow and can potentially ask questions. In short, it explains that each player has £10m to invest.

The second handout shows that there is a list of investment opportunities. Each player should choose an option at the beginning of every round. (Depending on the numerical ability of the class, they can split the money between different options – although the maths can get tricky at this point1). The level of return on investment depends on the roll of a dice which, again, is all explained on the handout. The player that makes the greatest return on £10m at the end of 6 rounds wins the game.

The learning

By challenging the students to make investment decisions, there is ample room for discussion on risk and opportunity cost. The choice of each option, for example, will carry a different risk and will also create an opportunity cost.

The numerical element provides a good test for calculating rate of return and, taken altogether, the activity provides a good basis for the question of why investors invest in businesses.

Ultimately, however, it is important to bring the discussion back round to the difficulty that underdeveloped countries have in raising finance. One task might be to get students to research whether the figures given in the handout are representative of the real world. Similarly, it might be worth exploring why people continue to invest their money in assets that yield a low interest rates as opposed to riskier (higher return options). There may even be scope for a discussion about the 2008 Great Recession and the importance of CDOs in the crash.#

Investment Game: Instructions

Give to students or read aloud

Background

You are living in the country of Rosaria. Rosaria is a underdeveloped country with an HDI of just 0.4. The currency of Rosaria is dollars.

You have managed to access some money (somehow - maybe you are the rich owners of some natural resources that Rosaria has). Your task is to decide how to invest this money.

How it works

You have $10million to invest.

The game will last for a period of 6 years. Each year you will be able to make an investment decision of where to put your money. The outcome (how much money you make) will depend on your choice and the roll of the dice.

Finally ...

The group that makes the most amount of money after 6 rounds, wins!!

Investment Game: The Options

The options to invest **each year** are as follows:

1. Rosarian banks offer a return of 6% on your savings at the end of the year. However, Rosarian banks are risky there is a 50% chance your money will go missing this year and you will lose it ALL to the corrupt bankers.

   (1-3 you lose everything; 4-6 you get 6%)

2. Rosarian stocks and shares. Returns will depend on their performance; there is an equal possibility of a -10% return, -5% return, 1% return, 5% return or a 10% return. There is also some chance someone will lose your shares in a 'bureaucratic error').

   (1 – lose everything. 2-6 corresponds to the figures above)

3. Government bonds. Currently these pay 11.25%. But, they are rated only just above Junk status by many of the credit-rating agencies (BBB-). There's a good chance that the Rosarian Government will default on these loans and you will lose a fair chunk of money (50%).

   (1-4 lose 50%; 5-6 gain 11.25%)

4. No questions-asked Swiss bank. Return guaranteed of minus 0.5% at the end of the year. These banks are very trust worthy!

   (no need to roll)

5. No questions-asked Cypriot Bank- return of 2% at end of the year. However, the Cypriot financial sector is very weak right now; in 2012 the Cypriot Government seized 10% of all financial assets owned by foreigners to help payback debt. There is a 1/6 chance HALF the money you have invested may be lost.

   (1 you lose 50%; 2-6 you get 2%).

Record your results here:

Year	Starting Amount	Option	Dice number	Finishing Amount
1	$10m			
2				
3				
4				
5				
6				
			Total	

www.ingramcontent.com/pod-product-compliance
Lightning Source LLC
Chambersburg PA
CBHW062337220526
45469CB00008B/2746